Clara Bates

From heart's content

Clara Bates

From heart's content

ISBN/EAN: 9783744736329

Printed in Europe, USA, Canada, Australia, Japan

Cover: Foto ©Thomas Meinert / pixelio.de

More available books at **www.hansebooks.com**

From Heart's Content

DEDICATION.

ONCE a dear house, beloved of pink sweet-
brier,
Beloved of woodbine, too, and then of fire,
Spread over you its blessed, sheltering eaves,
To whom I bring my handful of song-leaves—

A single handful. Now another roof,
Green, and with granite gables, low, aloof,
Is earth-home for you through the flying years,
To whom I bring my heart's love and my tears.

INDEX.

INDEX.

PROEM.

ACHILLES WITH HIS WOUNDED PRIDE.

A CHILLES, with his wounded pride,
　　Left the Greek tents, and by the sea
Sat down and told his injury
To Thetis, underneath the tide.

His brave soul surged with wrathful grief,
　　Resenting Agamemnon's wrong—
　　Did not the maid to him belong?
Why should he yield her to his chief?

The broad waves crowded to the sand,
　　Snow-white and green, and amethyst;
　　And Thetis, like a silver mist,
Came up and soothed him with her hand.

9

Oh, when by grief and loss opprest,
  My heart rebels against its fate,
  And lies within my breast a weight,
Of all, the sorest, heaviest,

In form of mist, or cloud, or flower,
  In shape of singing bird or bee,
  My Mother, Nature, comes to me,
And soothes me with her holy power.

WHITE VIOLETS.

A STAR fell from the sky at night,
  Through the dim stillness of the blue,
And sank, a transient gleam of white,
  Where beds of early violets grew.

It left no vacant place on high,
  It gave to earth no added light—
But flowers of color like the sky
  Were changed into a starry white.

DANDELION FASHIONS.

HERE and there—everywhere,
  Where the sun is, where the shade is,
Fresh and sweet on tip-toe feet,
  Stand the dandelion ladies;
Showy, gay, in spring array,
  Scores of dandelion ladies.

Green ruffs deck each slender neck;
  Every head has perched upon it,
Saucy, jaunty, made to flaunt, a
  Little yellow satin bonnet.
What a place for a pretty face
  Is a yellow satin bonnet!

This the style for a little while;
  Then, despite the time or weather,
All unite on a bonnet white,

Trimmed with a snowy pompon feather—
Puffy, fleecy, moonshine, breezy
    Thistle-fashioned tuft of feather.

Here and there—everywhere,
    Where the sun is, where the shade is,
Satin crown gives place to down—
    Fickle dandelion ladies!
Blows the wind, and who can find
    One of the dandelion ladies ?

CAPRICE.

"OH, dear me!" cried the April sky;
    "Oh, dear me—oh, dear me!
I feel as if I were going to cry
    At every cloud I see."
Then tears in a sudden flood ran down
Upon the world, so dusty and brown,
Till everything in field and town
    Was wet as wet could be.

"Oh, my! oh, my!" cried the April sky,
    As she bent above the sea,
"I cannot believe that horrid face
    With wrinkles looks like me!"
Then she laughed outright at her own frown,
And green grew the world that was so brown,
And all the shores and all the town
    Were bright as bright could be.

14

DID the robin—burnt-breast bird—
  When first from the South he came,
Whistle a hailing word,
  Or call a mystic name?

And was something, hidden dark
  Under the dead leaves, stirred?
And did it murmur, " Hark!
  My comrade's voice I heard?"

And rouse, and begin to grow
  With all the speed it might,
Until it had lifted—so
  This three-leaved flower white?

Wake-robin— white as the snow,
  In field and woodland place,
Nothing more fair can show
  To the northering sun its face.

THE BLUE BIRD.

A LEAF from the branching
　　Blue of the sky,
Came floating downward
From somewhere, up there
　　Very high.

The wind in a frolic
　　Blew it along,
From roof-peak to fence-post,
When, suddenly, vaguely,
　　We heard a song.

Like a fairy fife
　　It whistled clear,
Sweet to the heart
That throbbed to hear it,
　　Sweet to the ear.

A leaf sing—a leaf
   From the sky's blue tree?
A silver echo
Of songs that sunbeams
   Sing, maybe?

Ah, no,—'tis the bird
   That knows so well
When really and truly
The winter is going,
   And hastes to tell.

TRAVERSE TRAILING ARBUTUS.

THAT you should deem the place
   But a bleak sandy space,
Flowerless, desolate, little the wonder,
   Till you discover them,
   Stoop and uncover them,
Hidden so shyly their rusty leaves under.

   Not yet are skies serene:
   With but a breath between,
Sunshine comes after rain—rain sunshine
     follows;
   In their chill going, slow,
   Lingering wraiths of snow
Whiten the north hill-sides, haunt the low
     hollows.

   But with a sturdy cheer
   Comes this brave pioneer,

Daring the wilderness, glad in waste places;
    Indian in moccasin,
    Neighbor and next of kin,
Though in fair hue itself like the Pale-Faces.

    Housed in such dingy tent,
    Vagrant and indigent
Surely the dweller is. Be not too certain!
    All know what lovely eyes
    Look from the beggar's guise
In the wise fairy tales. Lift up the curtain!

    Never a maiden fair
    Come upon unaware
Flushed more the rose-leaf hues of Love's sur-
      prises;
    And the air redolent
    With a sweet, subtle scent,
Makes of the desert a garden of spices.

    Why all this beauty spread
    Here where no foot may tread?
All its pure mission vain, sadly you ponder.

Hark to the murmurings
Through the pine-needle strings!
Hark to the whispers of winds as they wander—

"Vain no created thing—
Bloom in sand; bird on wing,
Flying unnoted; nor water of ocean,
Though it forevermore
Beat on undiscovered shore;
Nay, nor the lightest cloud's airiest motion;

"Nay, nor the gems that shine
Deep in the deepest mine;
Nay, nor the dried leaf by Autumn breath
driven;
Nay, nor the unexpressed
Hope in the humblest breast,
Yearning, aspiring through darkness toward
Heaven!

"He who is Infinite
Watches with loving sight
Even obscure bud and dawn-tinted blossom,

Though never human eye
Seeks where they lowly lie,
Prayerful with perfume upon the earth's
bosom."

A FAIRY STORY.

I FIND my fairy stories in a book
  That all who choose may read:
Full of strange wonder to the eyes that look,
  And to the hearts that heed.

To-day the clouds have blotted out the blue;
  Mists hang upon the hill;
So here's a fairy story that is true
  To keep the children still.

A little thing flew through the summer air,
  On wings of misty white;
Loitered and faltered; then, none knowing
      where,
  Sank from her buoyant flight.

Either she found unwonted dew or green,
  And craved a brief delay,

Or suddenly some kindred hand was seen
  That beckoned her to stay.

She halted, stayed, nor evermore began
  That filmy flight again,
Nor was she missed by any eye of man—
  By wind or sun or rain.

The spot was on the grass beside the gate,
  Upon a quiet street,
Through which, day after day, early and late,
  Passed little children's feet.

And there, after a winter's ice and cold,
  After long weeks of snow,
Close to the daily beaten path, behold
  Something began to grow.

The children spied it, knew its pretty name,
  And what it promised knew;
And paused an instant as they went and came
  To see how fast it grew.

A dented leaf—from that called lion's tooth;
   A low bud, greenish-gray;
And then the flower, the dandelion, forsooth,
   So round, so yellow, so gay!

See it—the humble, shining little thing—
   Just what our tired eyes need.
The flying fairy of the misty wing?
   Ah, yes, that was the seed.

POKE BONNETS

SHALL I tell of a little lady
  Who, long time ago,
Went through a quaint old-fashioned garden,
  Tripping to and fro?

April airs were shivery, chilly—
  Walks were thawy, wet—
And scarce had a hyacinth or crocus
  Peeped a blossom yet.

But in a sunny, sheltered corner,
  This small lady knew,
Always first of the green things hast'ning,
  Early violets grew.

There, indeed, this morn she spied them,
  Hosts of tip-toe elves,
All through the beds and grassy borders,
  Out to sun themselves.

Crowds and crowds of the dainty creatures,
  Colored a grayish blue,
As if a bit of sky, in the twilight,
  Had fallen with the dew.

Happy her eager eyes to see them;
  Scanning each small head,
All of a sudden a thought came to her,
  And she, laughing, said:—

"Oh, you little, sweet poke bonnets,
  Now I see from where
Comes this tilted, comical fashion
  Of the one I wear."   •

This little lady—do you know her?
  Yes, she sits to-day
Here in her rocking chair—grandmother,
  Quiet and frail and gray.

While in the same old sunny corner,
  Tip-toe, every one,
Little poke bonnets crowd, delighted,
  Out to greet the sun.

THE LILAC.

THE sun shone warm, and the lilac said:
   "I must hurry and get
      My table spread,
For if I am slow, and dinner late,
      My friends, the bees,
         Will have to wait."

So delicate lavender glass she brought,
      And the dantiest china
         Ever bought:
Purple-tinted, and all complete;
      And she filled each cup
         With honey sweet.

"Dinner is ready," the spring wind cried;
      And from hive and hiding
         Far and wide,
While the lilac laughed to see them come,

The little gray-jacketed
Bees came, hum—m!

They sipped the syrup from every cell,
They nibbled at taffy
And caramel.
Then, without being asked, they all buzzed: "We
Will be very happy
To stay to tea."

THE MIRACLE.

LAST night the trees were bare
    When we looked out to see,
Against the sunset-colored air,
    Their complex tracery,
Like webs of fibred lace
    Between us and the sky,
With only roughly-budded trace
    Of leaves for by and by.

From twilight dusk to dawn
    There were no shocks nor jars
To show strange work was going on
    Under the watching stars;
No sound of bursting sheath,
    No rending of close chain—
Only a sudden risen breath
    Of cloud—a soft, sweet rain.

29

But see our maples now;
        They need another name!
Our elms, like last night's, bough for bough,
        Yet not at all the same.
More leaves are out than could
        The wildest numberer say—
Transfigured trees, a new-made wood,
        A resurrection day!

Yet this so quickly wrought—
        This instant, wondrous birth—
Grew by slow process, thought on thought,
        Out of the hiding earth.
Unseen and silent grew
        That now so glorifies.
What miracle can Love not do?
        O, read with grateful eyes !

THE DEARER LAND.

A LONG a sunny southern strand
   The drowsy water lapped the sand,
   As if had grown the wintry sea
Benign and friendly to the land.

A shimmering warmth was everywhere,
For soft as summer blew the air,
   Which, if it rustled in a tree,
Was sure to find a blue bird there.

One in his bright, sky-colored coat
Sat from his singing mates remote,
   Some saddening thought weighed on his mind,
And checked the warble in his throat.

"This all is fair, I know," he sighed,
"Still, there's a dearer land beside,

31

'Tis bleakly far, yet I could find
Its shelter, without light or guide."

Next day the listening pine trees heard
An argument of bird with bird.
    "Too early," many cried; but one:—
"It can no longer be deferred."

The many in their pleading failed;
The lonely, homesick one prevailed;
    And so, next morn, at rise of sun,
The airy fleet of blue wings sailed.

    *   *   *   *   *   *

Later. A Northern morning wild:
Out of her window looked the child;
    Flurries of snow were flying past;
Her casement ledge was heaped and piled.

She looked; and suddenly there flew,
Before her eyes, a fleck of blue.
    She cried with joy: "He's here at last—
I knew he'd come, I knew, I knew!"

He heard the voice, and turned to greet
The longed-for sound, so gay, so sweet,
    Nor heeded that the bough was cold
And snowy to his tender feet.

But sang with all his might and main:
"Ah, there's my little girl again;
    Ah, there she is—the Locks of Gold—
To greet me at the window-pane!"

THE MYSTIC VOICE.

THE wind blows south, and the wind blows
    west,
  And up on an apple-bough, just begun,
    Is a robin's nest.
And blue-birds look, as they flit and call,
  As if the cup of the sky, overrun,
    Some drops let fall.

The wind blows east, and the wind blows north,
  Yet crocus-heads, in their pretty caps,
    Are peeping forth.
Aimless white wings, the snow-flakes fly on,
  Then rest on a grass-blade, or perhaps
    On a dandelion.

Each has given a willing ear
  To some mystic sign, to some sweet "Hail!"
    That we do not hear.

And from far lands, and out of earth's prison,
Without delay, and without fail,
They sing, they are risen!

Oh, for an ear and a heart as willing
All still, small voices within to heed
To as sweet fulfilling!
To heed and doubt not: sure that Duty,
Though her ways may be dull and cold, will
lead
To Joy and Beauty.

HEYDAY, VIOLET.

HEYDAY, Violet,
  What did you hear
In your chill bed,
That you should be lifting
  Your shy head—
A silken snood
Knotted as would
  A Puritan maiden
Her blue hood.
And in your neck
  So lowly a crook,
That, however he tries,
Not once in your eyes
  Can the passer look?

  Ah, Violet,
I long to know,

But you'll not confess?
Then must I study,
  Ponder and guess.
Was the bird I noted,
Swift and song-throated,
  Of the color of sky
All winged and coated,
That hither flew
From the warm South,
As he passed you, mute?
Or with silver flute
  In his sweet mouth?

  Dear Violet,
So silent still?
  Then, if not the bird,
Still other voices
  Perchance you heard —
A dash and sprinkle
A rainy tinkle
  On the tin eaves,
While, with patter and wrinkle,
The puddles and pools

Were stirred to dance,
And with bubble feet
Did the whole wet street
Glisten and glance.

Or, Violet,
Spake there a sunbeam
    Through the mold,
King's messenger,
    With proffer of gold?
Largess outspreading,
In your lap shedding
    Coin and trinket,
    And ring for a wedding?
Or did a wind
    Pipe out of the west,
Call for you, claim you,
Of all maidens name you,
    Rarest and best?

Spake Violet:
" All those I heard,
    Nor was beguiled,

38

Nor waked, nor stirred,
   Till a little child,
   Laughing and merry,
   Step like a fairy,
      Searched for me, asked for me
   Eagerly, very.
Then I lifted my head,
   Shy though it be,
Out of the grasses,
That when she passes
   Her eyes will see."

THE APRIL SHOWER.

DOWN the drops come, tinkle, tinkle
  With a sudden dash and sprinkle,
Though as blue as periwinkle,
    Was the sky.

" Some mysterious hocus-pocus,
Knocked above us and awoke us,"
Cried a little yellow crocus,
    With a sigh.

There's a roaring, there's a clatter,
There's a smoky dash and spatter
Of the dust, as comes the patter
    Of the drops.

Such a drencher, such a pelter
Is it; yet when, helter-skelter,
Everything has found a shelter,
    Then—it stops !

THE HYACINTH BULB.

BEHOLD my bulb just putting forth a sheaf
   Of tender green from out its rusty bud !
Would the old Greeks have found upon its leaf
   " Ai, ai," and in its flower the young god's
      blood?

I find a sweeter message written there—
   No cry of woe, no hint of godhood slain,
But early promise of sun-flooded air,
   Warm, steaming earth and wind-blown, fra-
      grant rain.

Stored in this humble bit of clod there lies
   Such color as will glad all eyes, I know.
If bees love blue, then every bee that flies
   Will hasten to it when it comes to blow.

My heart, oft prone to question and to doubt,
   Says of this curious sphere, so brown, so dull:

"Soon spikes of blossoms will come bursting
out."
Says readily, "They will be beautiful."

Ah, since such easy task has Faith to trace
The future of this bulb from root to bloom,
Why should Hope flood with anguished tears
her face
Above her loved ones hidden in the tomb?

As from this germ a hyacinth will grow,
Sure as the springtime, sure as sun and rain,
Out of their blessed depths of sleep I know
In God's full season they will rise again.

AN EASTER FLOWER.

THROUGH all the winter chilly
  There slowly grew a lily,
From fresh bud thrust above the bulb,
  To soft expanding leaf,—
Though scant the sunshine that it felt,
  Long as the days were brief.

We knew a lovely blossom
  Was hid within its bosom,
And that its one green calyx sheath
  Did tenderly enfold
A snow-white flower, upon whose breast
  Would shine a dust of gold.

We watched, and, ah, we waited—
  It seemed so long belated;
We gave it freely light and drink,
  Though filled with fear and doubt;

Would ever that green prison burst
       And let its captive out?

       Behold on Easter morning,
       With no unusual warning,
Our lily stood in perfect bloom
       All gloriously white !
And thus our question had reply,
       Our doubt became delight.

       Out from its folded prison
       We felt it had arisen
To prove to us Life's narrowing bounds
       Will blossom and unclose,
Until the soul is freed and fair,
       As Christ himself arose.

THE FLAX BELLE.

FOREVER vain of her blue bonnet,
　　She nodded her silly head;
The summer wind blew soft upon it,
　　And this is what it said:—

" Dancing or spinning, which are you doing?
　　Lady Flax, with body slim
Here comes a worthy lover wooing;
　　Pray listen now to him."

On business bent, came humming over
　　A big commercial bee;
His dealings mostly were in clover
　　And a lively trade had he.

The pretty flax began coquetting,
　　Nodding her bonnet to him,

45

Until, his busy toil forgetting,
  He peeped beneath the brim.

" Which are you doing—dancing or spinning,
  Your foot so daintily trips?
My heart is lost in the very beginning,
  I beg to kiss your lips."

So boldly he pleaded a kiss, he won it—
  " No honey there!" he said—
" Only a bright blue flaunting bonnet
  On a little empty head."

So away he sailed, this work-day lover,
  Scorning the flimsy cheat;
In the plainer walks of weed and clover
  He found enough of sweet.

Cried the angry wind in a rising passion,
  " Lady Flax, with bonnet blue,
Never think with an idle fashion
  To hold a lover true."

A JUNE MERCHANTMAN.

A NCHOR weighed, adown the harbor,
With all her canvas spread,
And with steady prow and wake of murmur,
A small grey coaster sped.

Outward bound she was that morning,
On the sunny, blue-air sea;
Rudder to guide her hither, thither,
And fine gauze sails had she.

"Whither away, my bonny captain,
Whither away—away?
To Red-Rose land, or Pansy islands?
Or Hollyhock country gay?

"To the sleeping coast of scarlet Poppy?
To the Blue-flag's sluggish tide?

Or to the port where the Water-Lily,
  A gold-oared pinnace rides?"

" Nay, nay," cried the bonny captain,
  " I sail the blue-air sea
Straight for plain White Clover harbor,
  In the low Trefoil countree.

" I shall be loaded with pure sweet honey,
  And pure sweet wax for comb,
All that a small gray Bee should carry,
  When I come sailing home !"

THE POPPY.

WHEN first we spied it growing
    We thought it but a weed,
For no one that we knew of
    Had planted a poppy seed.

But suddenly where our weed was
    A crimson flower stood,
So dainty and bright we named it,
    Our little Red Riding Hood.

We said: "See how she carries
    That sweetly drooping head,
And the burnous upon her shoulders
    Is just the proper red.

"No doubt she is on her way now
    To grandmother's in the wood,
With cakes and a pat of butter—
    This little Red Riding Hood."

4

A cloud—of a hand's breadth only—
  A sudden, gusty stir—
And in one breezy minute
  Nothing was left of her.

Had a wolf come from the forest
  And caught her where she stood?
Ah, the wind was the wolf that ate her—
  Our little, Red Riding Hood.

THE BOBOLINK.

"HELLO," cried bobolink, "hello!"
As he ran up the stair
Of the sweet June air,
And called to a bee below:
"Say there, say there,
Bee, keep away there!
I am here to watch you,
Fly—or I'll catch you!"
And across the clover red
The bee fled.

Then bobolink laughed—"What fun!"
And further up the stair
Of the sweet June air
Climbed till he spied a hare run.
She now and then hurried,
Now and then tarried;

As he, loud and clear,
Shouted "Out of—out of here!"
Then swifter than the bee
Fled she.

The bobolink gurgled, "Ho, ho!"
And down the sunny stair
Of the sweet June air
He ran to his nest below.
Lady wife tittered,
While he bubbled, twittered,
"Big rabbit, little bee
Are both afraid of me!"
"'Tis because you are so noisy,"
Said she.

THE SPINNER.

A H, I think I hear a sound,
  Something humming round and round.
Is it wings astir, a flutter,
Just outside my window-shutter—
      Whir, whir,
Soft as old gray pussy's purr?

May be moth in foolish flight,
Lured here by my candle-light,
  Eager but to reach the burning
  Out of which is no returning,
      Soft of wing,
Newly-fledged and fluttering.

White the moon shines through the pane;
It is neither wind nor rain;
  But I'll see when morn uncloses,
  Fair and pink, my sweet-brier roses,

What it is
Makes such whirring sound as this.

Out I look upon the dawn,
Sound of spinning wheel is gone.
   Half unfolded roses cluster,
   And a web of silken luster
      Hangs and sways
In the early morning rays.

Did the spider make the whir
As she spun this gossamer?
   Patient, slow from the beginning,
   Real old-fashioned, great-wheel spinning,
      Thread by thread,
Back and forth with busy tread.

All I know is, something kept
Fluttering, rustling till I slept;
   And behold this fabric shining,
   White as mist with silver lining!
      I believe
I did hear her spin and weave.

A WEATHER PROPHET.

IT rains; this morning on a tree,
  We heard a low, shrill chirring;
We searched to find it carefully,
For well we knew the rogue must be
  A little tree-frog purring.

Blue as a larkspur was the sky;
  The bees went booming, humming;
While clouds like fair, slow ships sailed by;
No sign was there to any eye
  Of sudden rain-storm coming.

But chirr! he piped, and chirr! and chirr-r!
  The children sighed, "Provoking!"
Quite out of sorts, indeed, they were
That that small hidden thing should stir
  The sweet air with his croaking.

Their play was planned for out of doors
   When first they heard him calling,
And now a heavy darkness lowers;
Rain pattered first, and now it pours
   As if the sky were falling.

I fancy he will find some chink,
   With twigs and leaves for cover,
Where he can safely sit and blink,
And thrust his nose out for a drink,
   Until the rain is over.

You'd like to see him some fine day?
   Only quick eyes can find him.
He has a most mysterious way
Of being gray, if bark is gray,
   Green, if there's green behind him.

His guesses are not always right
   To the extent of bringing
A thunder rack of black in sight;
Yet sweet as the whistle of Bob White
   Is the little tree-frog's singing.

THE CHIMNEY SWALLOWS.

'TIS a puzzle indeed
I cannot read,
As to what is the earthly sense or need
For these little things,
With their swift wings,
To turn from the bough that tosses and swings,

And to choose as the best
Nook for a nest
The very last place one would have guessed,
When the summer tide,
So warm and wide,
Flows sunny and sweet on every side.

The chimney top! —
Nay, they do not stop
Even at that point, for down they drop —
Down out of the light,

Where 'tis dark as night,
And the soot is the only thing in sight.

Just think of a bird
That never heard,
As a baby, leaves above him stirred;
Nor the lullabies
Of the wind's soft sighs
To bring the sleep to his little eyes !

But instead, four grim
Black walls, and a dim
Far speck of the blue sky over him,
Are all he sees!
What sights are these
A little king of the air to please ?

Nor sound is here
For the song-tuned ear
Except the flight of the mother near.
His own sharp cries
Have for replies
But her common comfort of bugs and flies.

And when, ere long,

His wings grow strong,

And he flies with the rest of the twittering
throng,

How can he know

Which way to go,

Where all is dazzle and song and glow ?

If it fell to me

To suddenly see

So much strange color and life and glee,

Or fell to you,

What should we do ?

Why, I think perhaps we might fly too.

THE RUSHES.

SUCH fun the rushes have,
    With nothing else to do
But paddle, paddle in the water
    All the day through.

In a shallow pool
    By the river's brim,
There is room for thousands of them,
    They're so very slim.

All about their feet
    Crinkly ripples run;
Now and then a minnow swimmer
    Glances in the sun.

Hither, too, and thither,
    Right before their eyes—
Long and slender darning needles—
    Flit the dragon flies.

Do the rushes laugh?
   Yes, in their soft way;
And they whisper to each other
   All the time and say:

" Oh, isn't it fine fun
   With nothing else to do,
But paddle, paddle in the water
   All the day through?"

THE WATER LILY.

THE midnight face of the mountain lake
    A mask of silver wore,
With sombre locks of fern and brake
    Fringing the dusky shore.

I saw among the myriad stars,
    Floating therein serene,
A boat with golden masts and spars
    And oars of emerald green.

A merry chorus, low and sweet
    As the summer hum of bees,
And the graceful beat of dancing feet
    Came to me on the breeze.

It anchored—every gleaming oar
    Fell from the rower's hands;
The fairies lightly stepped to shore
    Upon the shining sands.

At morn I sought it—found not them
    Who gay moon-tryst had kept,
But moored upon its swaying stem
    A water-lily slept.

BY THE BROOK.

Bright in the sunny spaces,
Dark in the shady places,
Glides the brook with tinkling tones,
Over the smoothly-polished stones,
Lisps, and whispers, and seems to think:
"Run I must, run swift and cool,
For further on, by the quiet pool,
The thirsty grasses wait to drink."

Then as it onward passes,
Greetingly, meadow-grasses
Bow their long green bodies low.
"See, little brook, how fast we grow!
Nests, the cosiest, homelike things,
Hide with their young birds at our feet;
That is why, so noisy and sweet,
Bobolink with his neighbor sings."

Then from the waving cover,
    Bubbling, brimming over,
Bobolink flies up to shout
Some of his pent-up music out.
"I rise to tell you," he twitters fast,
    "If some of you are scared to hear
    The sound of a foot-fall drawing near,
Tis the dear little school-girl going past."

    She moves along the meadow
    Followed by fairy shadow,
That tries to be as light and fleet
As are her happy bounding feet.
Tinkles the brook from place to place,
    Nod the grasses, and sings the bird,
    As on she goes, with never a word,
But only a smile on her sunny face.

THE SPIDER WEB.

WHO but a fairy
  Ever lived in a house so airy?
A bit of cloud tied fast as it were,
And framed of the finest gossamer—
A wonderful, shining, silky house,
Swaying here in the sweet-brier boughs.
Sprite of some kind—Queen of the air—
Must needs be the one for a home so fair.

  Does she, I wonder,
Stand these pale-pink blossoms under,
Dressed in a skirt of vapory blue,
All spangled over with drops of dew?
Does she wear a crown, and in her hand
Carry aloft a long gold wand?
Has she wings to fly with, gauzy, green?
And where are the folk she rules as queen?

I look and linger,
And touch the web with careful finger;
When—in an eager, crafty way—
Out leaps a little gnome in gray!
The tiniest ogre that ever sate
And watched for prey at his castle gate:
His eight long arms so strong and bold
With which to seize, and strangle, and hold!

Should he discover
Some truant creature passing over—
A bee or fly on tired wing
Careless and fond of loitering,
I wonder if a mimic roar
Would reach its ears from out his door:
" Fe, fi, fo, fum!   Fe, fi, fo, fum!
I will have some!   I will have some!"

A FANTASY.

GOLD-RIBBED and silken-sailed from rose
to rose,
　With honey laden, fairy wild bees break
The currents of the air with steady prows,
　Leaving a surge of humming in their wake.

The wind sways with its music all the trees
　Whose leafy whispers make the bird-hearts
　　　beat;
While soft cloud-fleets sail heaven's azure seas,
　Vast phantom navies ride the billowy wheat.

Black water-spiders spin swift webs of light
　Moving upon the still face of the spring;
And bending ferns upon the pebbles white
　Their graceful forms in quiet shadows fling.

The fishes stirring in the water clear,
　Bind nets of sunlight on their golden scales;

68

The water-lilies ride at anchor near
　With sides of shining green and waxen sails.

I hear the tiny mermen's laughter sweet,
　Sporting the swaying water-weeds among,
And in the rustling brook are sounds of feet,
　Quick beat of drums and shouts of merry
　　song,

With click of many a pebble castanet
　As in an eager multitude they flee
Through the pure freshness of the rivulet
　On to the bitter, million-peopled sea.

JUNE.

OUT in the meadows clangor and din!
    Bobolinks jubilant over the clover,
Poised above it or hidden in;
Reeling, shouting song upon song—
    Shouting the same tune over and over,
Drunken with melody all day long.

Over the uplands, idle, cool,
    Truant winds with the sunshine wander,
Wrinkling the sleeping face of the pool—
Swaying the rose's graceful head
    That bends its blushing cheeks to ponder
The sweet false words the bees have said.

THE FIREFLIES.

WE watched the fireflies flashing
　　Through the dusk and dewy air,
Like a gleam of wandering lanterns,
　　Here and there.

"What bright-winged and jeweled creatures
　　Must those small things be," we said,
"May be gold and silver, may be
　　Burning red."

So we caught one, soft out-flashing
　　Near us, bore him tenderly
To a light within, that better
　　We might see.

Well, and was his body golden,
　　Gilded round with burnished rings?
And did quills of silver feather
　　Make his wings?

71

No; we found our fine light-giver
  Just a small, plain, gray-brown fly,
With no outward sign of splendor
    To the eye.

And we thought one cannot always
  Take the garment as a sign
Of how far and bright some inner
    Light may shine.

THE WASP'S HOUSE.

YOU call them hateful little things,
    Whose airy wings
Bear them aloft, as a thistle's crown
Is blown by a zephyr up and down.
You fly with dread, or shrink with fear
If one of them simply pauses near.

See here, beneath the vine-hung eaves,
    Where trailing leaves
Hide it, as if it had not been,
Is the little house the wasps live in;
Made of wonderful paper, gray,
As if worn by the weather many a day.

I wonder what would be inside,
    If open wide,
Upon noiseless, silken hinges hung

Some secret door or casement swung,
And we such a hasty glance might cast
As a swallow does in sailing past.

Would we see a fairy palace, where
      A silver stair
Of filigree wire runs to seek,
Through many a story, the topmost peak,
And the spacious rooms and vaulted halls
Have floors of wax, and waxen walls?

Or would it be a prison grim,
      Where heavy and dim
The air is ever with sounds of pain,
Of bolt and bar and of prisoner's chain;
And where the captives, held to die,
Are shrunken of limb and sad of eye?

Ah, neither; listen the harmless hum,
      As go and come
Those little people, who, day by day,
Have toiled and wrought with the paper gray !
Nothing of mystery is in this;
But only a simple Home it is.

And cheerily, with the sweet bread
        Of honey fed,
Therein the young ones wait their wings.
And though we may think wasps hateful things,
Yet surely we must have the grace
To own that their house is a cosy place.

MORNING.

THE doors that night had barred with dark,
Morn opens with a golden key,
And in her lightning-winged barque
Comes flashing o'er the sea.

Heaven, with her dusky mask thrown off,
Smiles gloriously to see her come;
Waves, whispering of her beauty, doff
Bright caps with plumes of foam.

Gray mists steal backward at her glance;
Breezes leap up, to wake and stir
The June leaf-pulses, in a dance
That shakes the gossamer.

The lips of Silence part to sing:
And startled Echo's thousand throats,
Mid hum of bee and flash of wing,
Repeat the wondrous notes.

Oh, Morn of Hope, within my soul,
   That bursts the bonds of grief and doubt,
Thus let all gladness inward roll
   As night and fear go out!

.

HARVEST MOONSHINE.

THE round moon comes from the distant seas
　　With a silvery softness in her light,
And the dusky trunks of the forest trees
　　Gleam, pillars of marble, tall and white.

The hill crouches down 'neath the sky's cool
　　　calm,
　　With its tawny mane of ripened wheat,
Like a lion under a towering palm
　　After its chase in the desert heat.

CLAD IN GRAY.

A LITTLE housewife bee,
  Fussy and gray was she,
Hummed at the clover tops continuously.

The summer day was fair,
And through the sunny air,
The birds on breath of song soared every-
where.

She had no colored coat,
No gold band at her throat,
Nor painted wings to flutter with or float.

A sort of grizzled fur
Wrapped and encompassed her,
Except her wings of faded gossamer.

79

Her voice was low and fine;
I heard her drone and whine;
I saw her heedless of the song and shine;

And yet it seemed that none
Under that summer sun
Was any happier than this busy one.

The idle and the gay
Went on their careless way,
Nor noted the little housewife clad in gray;

And yet, I thought, how sweet
The honey she could eat:
How cool the clover must be to her feet !

The wholesome element
Of Labor's true content
Was through her humble, plodding presence
    lent

To a day otherwise
Given to butterflies,
That fluttered but to vanish from the eyes.

THE QUAIL.

WHEN the fields were ripened
And the woods were red,
To her little flock of chickens
Mother Quail said:
"Here's a lesson for you!
Be sure you say it right,
Whistle, now whistle—
Bob, Bob, White !"

"Oh, mother dear," they quavered
"That's the name, perhaps,
Of the roving farmer boy
Who sets quail-traps !
If we sing together,
Out he might run,
To shoot your little children
With his dreadful gun !"

6

Mother Quail was troubled,
She glanced at the sky:
"Clouds are rather black, I think
'T will rain by and by.
So here's another lesson
That is better yet,
Whistle, now whistle—
More, more wet."

GRASS GIPSIES.

WHY, here is a camp,
  On the wayside grass !
Let's look at the tents
  Before we pass.
Beaded with dew
  Is every one --
Ah, 'tis only webs
  The spiders have spun.

They are gipsies. Think
  When night fell down,
How they set to work,
  So tiny and brown,
To pitch these tents —
  Each gathering boughs
To kindle a fire
  Before his house.

How a grandmother sat
　Under the flap
Of a tent, and rocked
　A babe in her lap !
And how on a stick
　A kettle was hung,
That to cook their supper
　Bubbled and sung.

How swarthy youths
　Took their guitars,
And played serenades
　To the far stars;
And shadows danced wildly
　All about,
Till the low red fire
　Had faded out !

ON AN OCTOBER THISTLE.

UGH! Shriveled and cold,
   Bald-headed and old,
They stop at a thistle-top to warm—
   The burly wingers,
   The honey singers,
The veterans left from the summer swarm.

   First Bee:—Ah, me!
   To have lived to see
Gray hairs and grief and poverty!
   To have grown so old
   That my bands of gold,
Bright yellow once, are dim with mold!

   I, such a fop
   That I could not stop
At any but snow-white clover-top,
   To bow my head,

85

And beg for bread
From only a common weed, instead !

Second Bee:—Hello !
Why, I've let go !
My fingers fail, they have weakened so.
The most to be said
Of this thistle-head,
As a first-class inn, is, that it's red.

Why, in my day,
To have come this way,
Was to meet all Bee-dom, blithe and gay.
There was all the sweet
That we could eat,
But *now*—Hello! I've lost my feet !

Third Bee:—Egad!
Zounds! but I'm mad,
Such a wretched time as I have had.
My voice has grown
Hoarse as a bone,
That once was the silveriest baritone.

Indeed, it's rough
To bark and cough,
Till the skin of one's throat is all worn off.
And to be pointed out
As having the gout,
Because I have grown a little stout !

So, there they pined,
And droned and whined,
And grumbled and buzzed till the sun went
down.
Next day—alas !
Upon the grass
Lay three little shrunken tufts of brown.

THE CRICKET'S TALE.

"GOOD morning, Mr. Cricket,
  How did you sleep last night?
Sure, never was the sky so clear,
  The moon so big and white.
I listened to the concert
  Your friends gave. Certainly
They played with more than usual skill
  That blue-grass symphony."

He sat in the sunshine, rubbing
  His arms and back and knees,
And shook his bulgy head and sighed:
  "Don't ask me, if you please,
For I never closed a winker!
  We played the concert through,
Though I scraped those blessed fiddle-strings
  Up to my chin in dew.

"My friend with the hurdy-gurdy,
  And the one with the flageolet,
The bagpipe man and the bugle-blower
  Were drenched and dripping wet.
And just in the very thickest
  Of baritone and bass,
A misty, ghostly-looking thing
  Came stealing by the place.

"I felt a chill like the ague
  Go crawling up my spine;
And my neighbor with the castanets
  Begged for a sip of wine;
And the tenor in his solo
  Coughed between every note,
And the little soprano lady tied
  A kerchief round her throat.

"The pipes whined shrilly, feebly;
  One quaver the bassoon blew;
Then all, as if of one accord
  Stopped short, and shuddered, 'Ugh !'

Not another chirrup they ventured,
    Jingle, tinkle or clink!
Now, who was that misty, ghostly thing?"
    I said, "Jack Frost, I think."

METEORS.

IT snows—for whitely through the dark
    And silence of the autumn night
Has fallen many a gleaming spark;
    And yet the meadows are not white.

Late flowers bow their heads in sleep;
    With plaint the night bird keeps awake;
The moon swings on her light lines deep
    In the blue waters of the lake.

The wind sobs fitfully; the trees
    Weep faded leaves to prove their woe,
That once in answer to the breeze
    But song-notes gave and whispers low.

Yet skies are clear—it is not snow,
    No cloud frowned from the face of even—
But weeds the hands of angels throw
    From out the star-flower garden, Heaven.

FRINGED GENTIANS.

SO long had the October skies
Worn frown of cloud and rain,
It seemed as though my tired eyes
Would never see again
What they so loved—the tender hue
Of heaven's own blue.

I watched in vain for brightening streaks
As dawned or died the day;
But still the distant mountain peaks
Wore cowls of misty gray;
Nor gleamed one shining hand-breadth through
Of heaven's own blue.

I sought a lonely country road,
With bare fields at each side,
Where late the golden-rod had glowed
In all its plumy pride—

Lo, something at the wayside grew
      Of heaven's own blue.

Fringed gentians—each one bearing up
      Atop its humble stem,
As with an arm aloft, a cup;
      I paused to look at them—
As deep a tint they wore, as true
      As heaven's own blue.

I had so missed the sky's dear face,
      Its color and its light;
Yet here in this deserted place
      Was something just as bright—
The bluest thing I ever knew
      Except heaven's blue.

Thus, often when the joys of earth
      Are dimmed, or disappear,
Lo, humbly in the wayside dearth
      We find some other cheer—
Some lowly flower that wears the hue
      Of heaven's own blue.

INDIAN SUMMER.

AUTUMN—an Indian red and old,
  Whose heart was throbbing faint and
    slow,
Wished ere it grew forever cold
  To be at peace with all below.

Round the frost-kindled council-fire
  Gathered the tribes from far and near;
Last words this dying chief and sire
  Would speak that day, and all must hear.

His weak hand grasped a calumet—
  A reed for stem, a red clay bowl,
The whole with bits of feather set—
  He filled it—lit it with a coal,

Then spake to them: " My race is run:
  My feet—no longer swift—are bound

Far past the setting of the sun
  Into the happy hunting ground.

"So warriors, brothers, braves, to-day
  Our hands will meet, our strifes will cease.
Smoke with me in last friendly way
  This pipe—this calumet of peace.

"Now I have done."   His gray head bent
  As bends a corn-ear fully ripe,
And round the dusky circle went,
  From lip to lip, the lighted pipe.

Up from the forest council-fire
  A cloud of azure vapor broke,
Veiled with soft haze the sky entire,
  And mantled all the earth with smoke.

THE WHITE DEER.

I LOOKED upon a cloudless night
  And saw a white deer bounding past
Where fetters of the cold moonlight
  Held all the forest shadows fast.

His hoofs were silver, and they beat
  So silently the dewy sod,
I said: "They're shod like goblin feet;
  At morn I'll find the path they've trod.

"The jewel-weed and asters grow
  In tangles by the river's brink,
This is his run-way, and I know
  He's going there to graze and drink."

When the first sunbeams ran—alas!
  The pathways where the white deer crossed,
I found upon the glistening grass
  The foot-prints only of the Frost.

GOLDEN-ROD.

AN idle breeze strayed up and down
   The rusty fields and meadows brown,
  Sighing a grievous sigh: "Ah, me !
  Where can the summer blossoms be?"
When suddenly a glorious face
Shone on him from a weedy space,
   And with an airy, plumy nod,
   "Good afternoon," said Golden-Rod.

  The breeze received her courtesy,
And then came hurrying home to me,
   And eagerly this story told:
   " I've seen a lady dressed in gold,
So shining that the very light
That touches her is doubly bright—
   She nodded, too, a royal nod."
   "Why, that," I said, " is Golden-Rod."

"Come out and see her where she stands,
Gold on her head and in her hands,"
   He cried; and I without delay
   Went after where he led the way;
And there she stood, all light, all grace,
Illumining the weedy place,
   And to us both, with airy nod,
   "Good afternoon!" said Golden-Rod.

THISTLE DOWN.

NEVER a beak has my white bird
    Nor throat for song,
But wings of silk by soft wind stirred,
  Bear it along.

With wings of silk and a heart of seed,
  O'er field and town,
It sails, it flies—some spot has need
  Of a thistle down.

A FOGGY MORNING.

A SMALL, close world it seems to-day,
  With fog about us, chill and gray,
As if had giant spiders spun
  Their webs between us and the sun,
Nor any wind had strength to stir
  Their leagues on leagues of gossamer.

Dim shapes of elm and locust wait
  Like shadowy sentinels at the gate;
They outline 'gainst the ghostly white
  The utmost limit of our sight;
There are no streets, no passers-by,
  No spire, no mountain-peak, no sky.

And yet a strong wind rushing forth,
  With cool fresh breath, from out the north,
Would part this cobweb vail in twain

And bring the sweet world back again—
The blue of sky, the fervid sun,
And all bright things he shines upon.

OCTOBER.

L EAPS October from the ashes dead
  Of the radiant, glowing-souled September !
Now the sun burns in the heavens, red
  As an angry eye, or a far ember.

To the sky the giant groves of oak
  Arms of dull bronze, acorn-hung, are raising;
Poplars all are dimly white like smoke;
  All the sumach's minarets are blazing.

Ripe nuts hang upon the bending trees,
  Like the pendant heads on lily anthers,
Squirrels, springing, shake them like a breeze—
  Squirrels, black or tawny, lithe as panthers.

Deer look into wild eyes as they drink,
  Eyes all dark and soft and clear, with wonder;

Wrinkled waters make the rushes shrink—
   Break their shadowed lengths of green
      asunder.

Crickets clang their black metallic wings,
   Drowning insect pipings, shrill and slender;
Tardy bees, begirt with golden rings,
   Hum around the garden's faded splendor.

All the year's sweet heats and growths are fled;
   All its days are sad; and changed and sober
All its golden glow, its burning red,
   As it wanes toward winter, through October.

AUTUMN RAIN.

I WATCH, the while my window-pane
  Is drenched with chilly tears,
To see if once the weather-vane
  Turns from the East, or veers;
But blurring, blinding, falls the rain
  Until the twilight nears.

And then across the stormy sky
  I see a brightening rift;
Like wings almost too weak to fly,
  The gray clouds slowly drift,
Till suddenly my waiting eye
  Beholds them rise and lift;

Uprise, uplift, till they disclose
  The old-time, tender blue,
Like a vast azure lake, that shows
  Bright islands scattered through—

Islands of purple, pearl and rose,
　And every sunset hüe.

If but the thrushes lingered yet,
　How surely should we hear,
From some tall tree-top in the wet,
　Their music sweet and clear,
Ready all darkness to forget
　Soon as the light shines near.

But days are short, and birds are few;
　And leaves let go their hold
From frosted twig and bough, to strew
　The ground with faded gold;
And long ago the songsters flew;
　The year is growing old.

Be thou, then, Heart, the thrush to sing!
　Take on thyself that part,
Though heavy with much sorrowing,
　And doubts, and cares, thou art.
Fair morrow will red sunset bring;
　Sing gratefully, O Heart!

HOAR FROST.

WAKE early, Gold Locks, come and look !
   The grass is all a shining white,
      As if above it in the night
Their wings a flock of snow-clouds shook

And scattered here and there a plume !
   Or, rather, white, as I have seen
      Upon it, in its first young green,
The fallen showers of orchard bloom.

A winter crisp is in the breeze,
   A winter dazzle on the lawn,
      As, flushed and summer-like, the dawn
Comes up from out its crimson seas.

The keen frost-crystals, starlike, plain,
   Vanish before it from our view,
      First they become a shower of dew,
And then a dripping shower of rain.

'T were lovely, if we need not know
    That in an hour the aster beds,
    With all their purples, all their reds,
Such blackening change must undergo;

And that the woodbine, which has grown
    Of late so like a kindling flame,
    Bent, as if overcome with shame,
Will all its loosened leaves drop down.

Somehow, the autumn signs dismay
    With symbols the foreboding heart,
    Since Life sees its own counterpart
Always in blossom and decay

Ah, child,—my fancy runneth so—
    Time's dread hoar-frost, as white and cold
    As this, must some day touch the gold
That has such live, bright overflow

Upon your little head—almost
    Too shining and too warm a braid
    It seems now, as it hangs, to fade
Under the touch of any frost!

Yet will it come, I know.   But when
        This ruddy color silvered is
        I may not be where I shall miss
Its tender earthly sunshine.   Then

Heaven shall, perhaps, have satisfied.
        And you, in that far time, which seems
        Too distant even for my dreams,
Will have your own dear fireside;

Perhaps a little grandchild, too,
        Which you will guard with heart and eyes—
        As now the two gray heads you prize
And love, so watch and cherish you.

*   *   *   *   *   *

See ! while in reverie Fancy hath
        So fleetly run to that far land,
        Upon whose vague, untrodden sand
She fain would trace your future path,

The aster stalk has bent its crown
        Of purple, or of red, indeed,
        While slowly, as if wounds did bleed,
The woodbine leaves are dropping down.

AUTUMN SUNSET.

EACH tree-top waved a crimson crest,
   A burning belt bound every spire,
As on the hearth-stone of the west
   The evening lit its glowing fire,

Warm, red; then backward seemed to gaze
   Upon the earth, as one would turn
From his own cheerful parlor blaze
   To watch the street lamps dimly burn.

The fire died out; then chill winds blew
   The clouds, like ashes gray and white,
About the air; in dark and dew
   Came down the gloomy autumn night.

A TWILIGHT MOUSE.

WOULD you think a mouse could fly—
    A mouse with soft, bright eye,
    Clothed in a gray-brown wrap
    Of fur, or silk, mayhap,
And with clinging, claw-like feet,
And heart with a panting beat?

No doubt you are wont to think
Mice live in a cupboard chink,
    And only in crannies creep,
    To scurry, and blink and peep;
To nibble at things, or gnaw
With white teeth sharp as a saw.

But if not a mouse, what then
Is this twilight denizen,
    That, without quill or feather,
    Has suddenly fluttered hither,

110

And that we, I scarce know how,
Have made our captive now?

It is nothing to shudder at;
It comes with the dusk—the bat.
  It likes the shadows' hue;
  It likes the smell of the dew;
And perhaps is fond of the far
Sky-gleam of moon or star.

Awkward? hideous?—look
At the end of each wing a hook!
  These are its fore-feet, see
  It walks so curiously.
And its black nose?   Well, I own
It does look upside down.

Feel now how like a drum
Its tiny heart's wild thrum!
  And see how the lamp's light
  Dazzles its purblind sight—
Poor little throbbing thing,
Give it its silken wing!

And when next dusk you spy
A flitting thing go by,
  Think, "That is our prisoner,
  The bat with mouse-like fur
And vellum wings, that goes—
Whither, nobody knows!"

NOVEMBER.

DAMP is the air with coming snow;
 In rustling flocks the dead leaves blow
Like birds a chilly storm-wind beats.
I watch, through the imprisoning glass,
The muffled people, hurrying, pass
 Along the windy streets.

I have my will, but not my way,
Else were the distant meadows gay
 With clover bloom and bumble-bees;
The dun wheat stubble-lands were seen
Rolling their billows, glistening, green,
 To counterfeit the seas.

These dull low skies of threatening hue
Were hung with banners broad and blue;
 Or black, and sharply cloven in twain

8

With lightning like a sabre's flash,
Shaken with answering thunder crash,
    Were spent in sweet warm rain.

Each green bough swung its singing bird;
Each living creature had its word
    Of happy love, or joy, or praise;
Were all that flood of sunshine back,
Unfelt were the wild loss and lack
    Of these November days.

I have my will, but not my way,
Else Yea were the great barrier Nay
    That frowns between me and the Light;
The future of my dreams were here;
Hope's far, faint glory dazzled near
    And full into my watching sight;

Work fell to none but the able hand;
After brave effort, ample, grand,
    Came the achievement!—Vain my one
Weak, human protest; better pray :
"When my will thwarts Thy righteous way,
    Ever Thy will be done !"

DARK DAYS AND FAIR.

ONE day goes clouded to its close,
At setting dull as when it rose;
Another has the sunny blue
Arched over it from dew to dew;
More have their mingled phases—rare
The wholly dark or wholly fair.

So lives their little orbits run
Either in shadow or in sun.
This glad one, noonday tempests smite;
This sad one, evening glories light
With unexpected radiance. Rare,
The wholly dark or wholly fair.

But Faith has wings for any sky!
Send her abroad her powers to try
When the uplifting airs are warm,

That, should her flight encounter storm,
With trial made strong, her wings may dare
Boldly alike the dark and fair.

Secure the soul that rests on Faith !
Upborne as by an animate breath,
She soars beyond earth's loss and gloom,
Beyond the shadow of the tomb,
With rapture, where is Heaven's free air
Wholly unclouded, wholly fair !

THE SQUIRREL'S WIGWAM.

THEY laid it low,
Row upon row,
The tall straight corn that rustled so.
Its once rank green was dry and sere—
Stalk, leaf-blade, tassel, silk and ear
Shriveled—and of its waving grace
Only a stiffened, ghostly trace.

The work all done
That rain and sun
Had lavished such sweet care upon !
The long ranks where the summer wind
Could walk, and clouds their shadows find,
Gathered, and set in shocks to stand
Lifeless, to wait the husker's hand !

117

Yet presently
A new degree
Of grace that cornfield had for me.
One shock was a true wigwam shape,
The long leaves just the things to drape
About the tent-poles, shelter fit
For what live thing might live in it.

Now, what if through
Some chink, a blue,
Faint smoke-puff should go up, and you
Should spy a red-man, with a deer
Slung on his shoulder, drawing near;
A leather belt, knives dangling there
And eagle feathers in his hair ?

A startling phase
Of wild-wood ways
'Twould be for these tame modern days;
But I see something which to me
Is quite as interesting—he,
That fine fox squirrel, running fleet
Towards it with his spry, small feet.

He'll find the door,
Be sure ; and more
He'll find the gold corn-ears in store.
And till the huskers come to tear
His wigwam down, will scamper there,
In, out, small red-man, saucy, slim,
As if the place were made for him.

THE FIRST SNOW.

WITH dull-red splendor in his gaze,
    The sun sank to his nightly rest,
And clouds whose rims were all ablaze
    Piled mountain-high with gloom the west.

Without the sunset's golden flush
    To crimson o'er the winter sky—
To make the leafless tree-tops blush,
    The fields in burning glory lie;

To wander lonely wilds about,
    Each lowly hut from gloom to win,
Making a warm fire glow without
    Where warm fires never glowed within;

To wind a thread of silver light
    Where streams, locked in an icy hold,

Lay whitely 'mid the forest's blight,
　　Their lips of music dumb and cold—

Nature was desolately drear,
　　And told in wailings loud and deep
A tale of hopeless woe and fear,
　　As, wrapped in clouds, she sank to sleep.

But when the monster Cyclops, Day,
　　Shaking the dun locks from his brow,
Opened his great dull lid of gray,
　　The world was beautiful with snow.

THE ROBIN'S FAREWELL.

GOOD-BYE, old tree, good-bye !
   I leave my nest with you;
You'll need it when your green leaves die,
   And your apples are fallen too;
Something upon your boughs
   For children to come and see,
If only a bird's deserted house—
   Good-bye, old apple tree !

We were friends from the very first,
   When in the chill March air,
Before a single bud had burst,
   I found you bleak and bare.
Even then your branches stirred
   In a kindly, welcoming way,
As if they knew a lonely bird
   Needed some place to stay.

And after that you spread
  The greenest, leafiest roof
That ever sheltered a robin's head,
  Waving, but weather-proof.
And I remember well
  How every gala breeze,
Before your pink-white blossoms fell,
  Brought scores of honey bees.

They hummed their drowsy tune;
  My mate sang loud and sweet;
And the sun winked, and the quiet moon
  Walked by with silver feet;
While with my mother-wings
  I brooded the eggs of blue,
Till those four red-breast little things
  Grew restless and broke through.

You rocked them every one;
  But now, in the usual way,
They have learned to fly, and would be gone,
  And so, we are off to-day.

More than they dream of now
   They'll miss your lullaby,
Miss every leaf, and twig and bough—
   Good-bye, old tree, good-bye !

THE FOUR WINDS.

THE wind of the south
    Comes over the land,
With a flute in her mouth
And a dandelion
    Within her hand.

Like a giant to wrestle
    Is he of the North,
Yet a boy to whistle
In chimney and keyhole
    When he goes forth.

The wind of the West
    Is a gentle soul,
And rocks the nest
And the yellow fledgelings
    Of the oriole.

Cries the East to the vane,
　　"No time to lose,
It is going to rain,
Get out your umbrella
　　And overshoes !"

Now, which of these
　　Do you like the best—
The blue-bird's breeze,
The giant whistler,
　　The East or the West?

SUNDOWN.

THE day begins to doze:
    Her wide blue eyes are tired of light,
The sun has glared so fierce and bright.
So, drawing close her cloudy cap
About her forehead for a nap,
From out her western sleeping-place,
She smiles " Adieu," her broad fair face
    Red as a rose.

    The world of fleece-white snow
Grows gray and chill; but in the sky
Winks here an eye and there an eye—
Winks, blinks, then stays, a keen cold spark,
To watch the sullen stealthy dark
Out of its cavern rise and drift,
As if a river black and swift
    Did overflow.

Slowly, and not too soon
To make her radiance the surprise
And glory of the waiting skies,—
A silver kite on viewless line,
Or bubble blown to soar and shine,
Shedding the hoar-frost of her rays
Broadcast in one wide luminous haze,—
Rises the moon.

www.ingramcontent.com/pod-product-compliance
Lightning Source LLC
Chambersburg PA
CBHW030618270326
41927CB00007B/1218